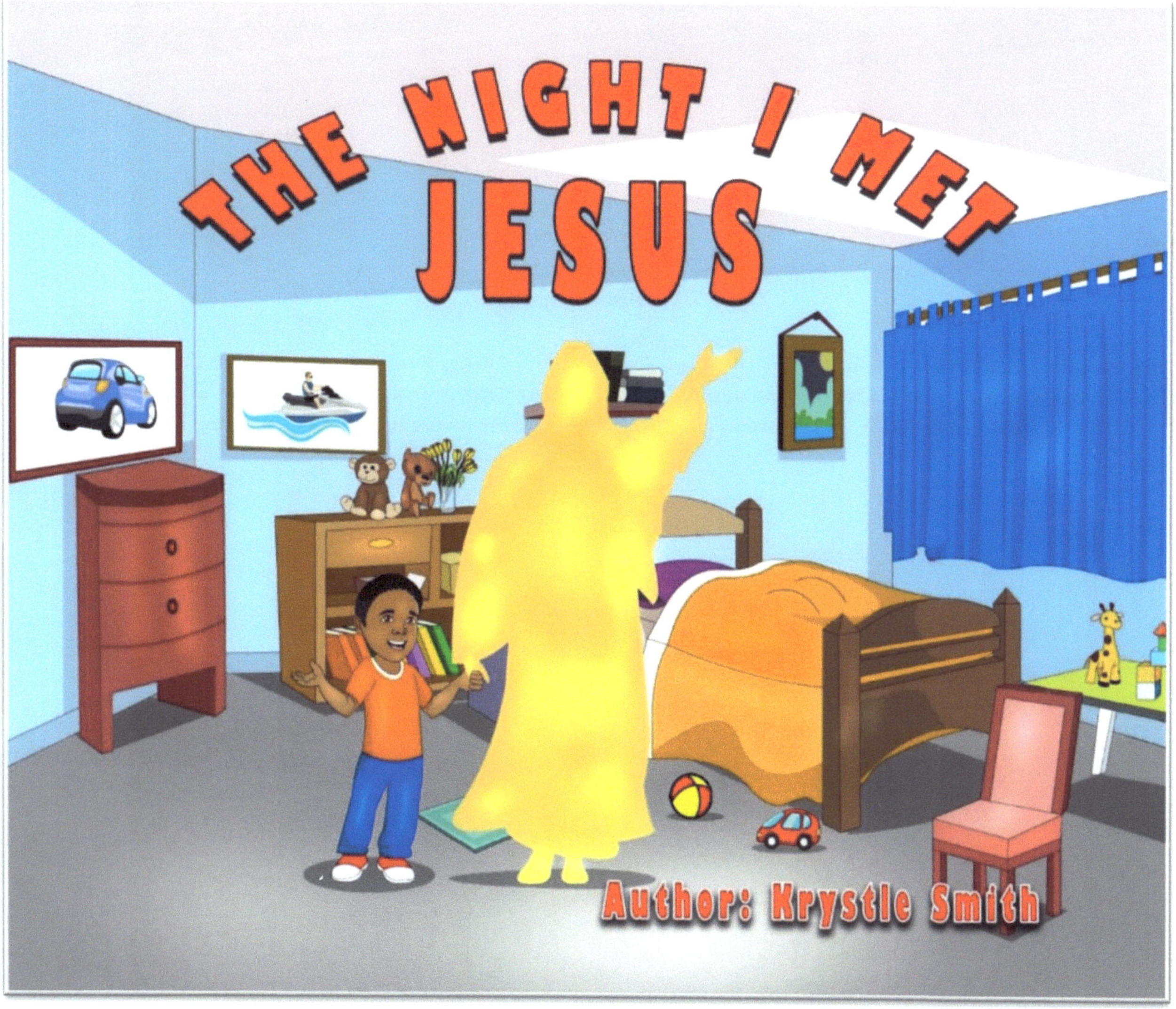

Written & Illustrated by Krystle Smith
Copyright © 2019
Krystle Smith
The Night I Met Jesus
All rights reserved.

No part of this publication may be reproduced, distributed, or transmitted in any form or by any means, including photocopying, recording, or other electronic or mechanical methods, without the prior written permission of the publisher, except in the case of brief quotations embodied in critical reviews and certain other non-commercial uses permitted by copyright law.

Krystle Smith
Krystle_S_Smith@yahoo.com

Printed in the United States of America
First Printing 2019
First Edition 2019

10 9 8 7 6 5 4 3 2 1

The Night I Met Jesus is a children's book.

This Book Belongs To:

_____

The Night I Met Jesus

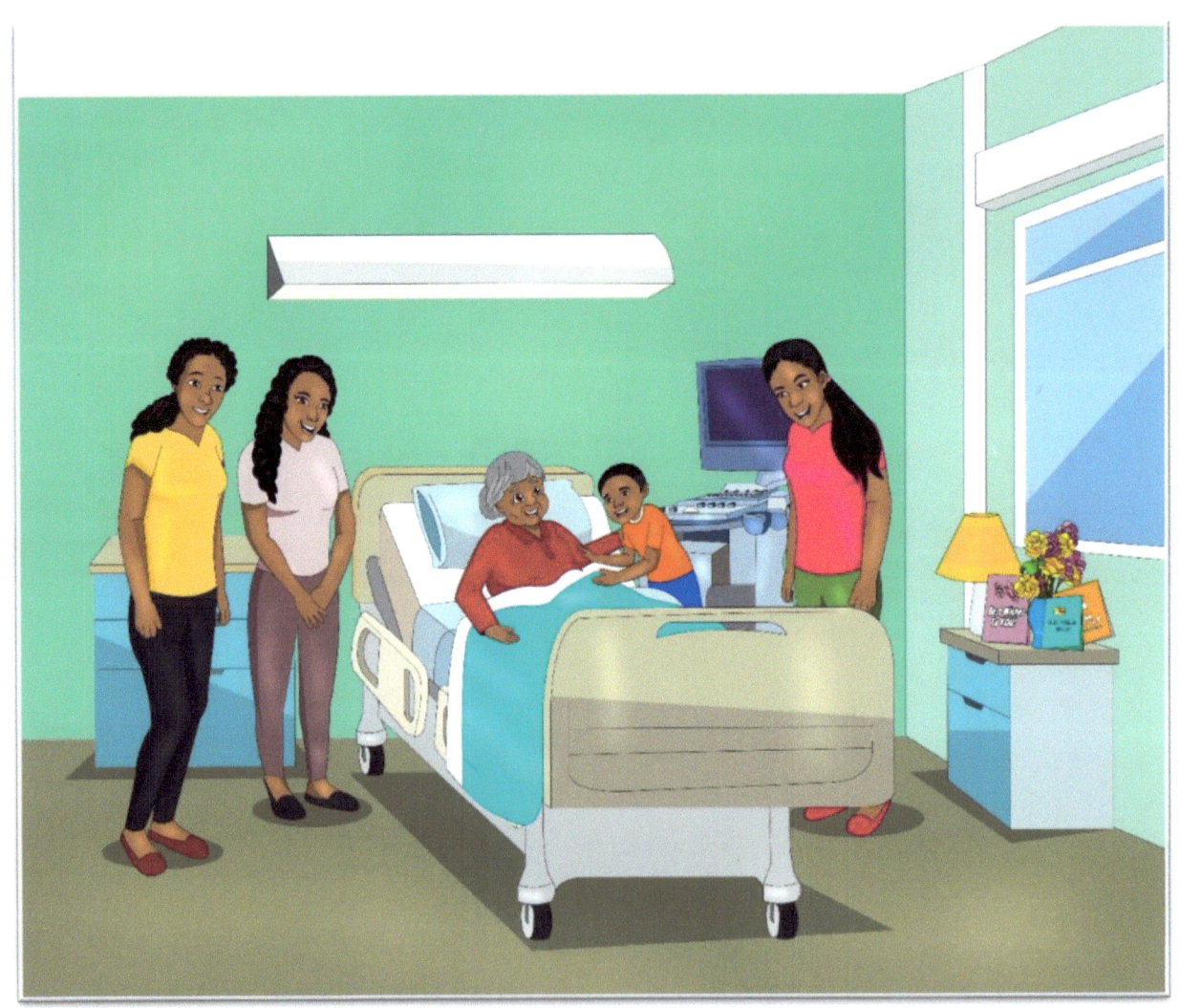

1. The Night I Met Jesus

Hi, grandmother! How are you? Oh son, I'm doing fine. I'm glad to see you're doing better, grandmother I really miss you, oh honey, I miss you as well, (as she reaches to gives him a hug.) I can't wait 'til you come home, because I have a lot of things planned for us to do.

As she chuckles she says, "oh really? "Yes, really, "Sheldon replied with a smile on his face.

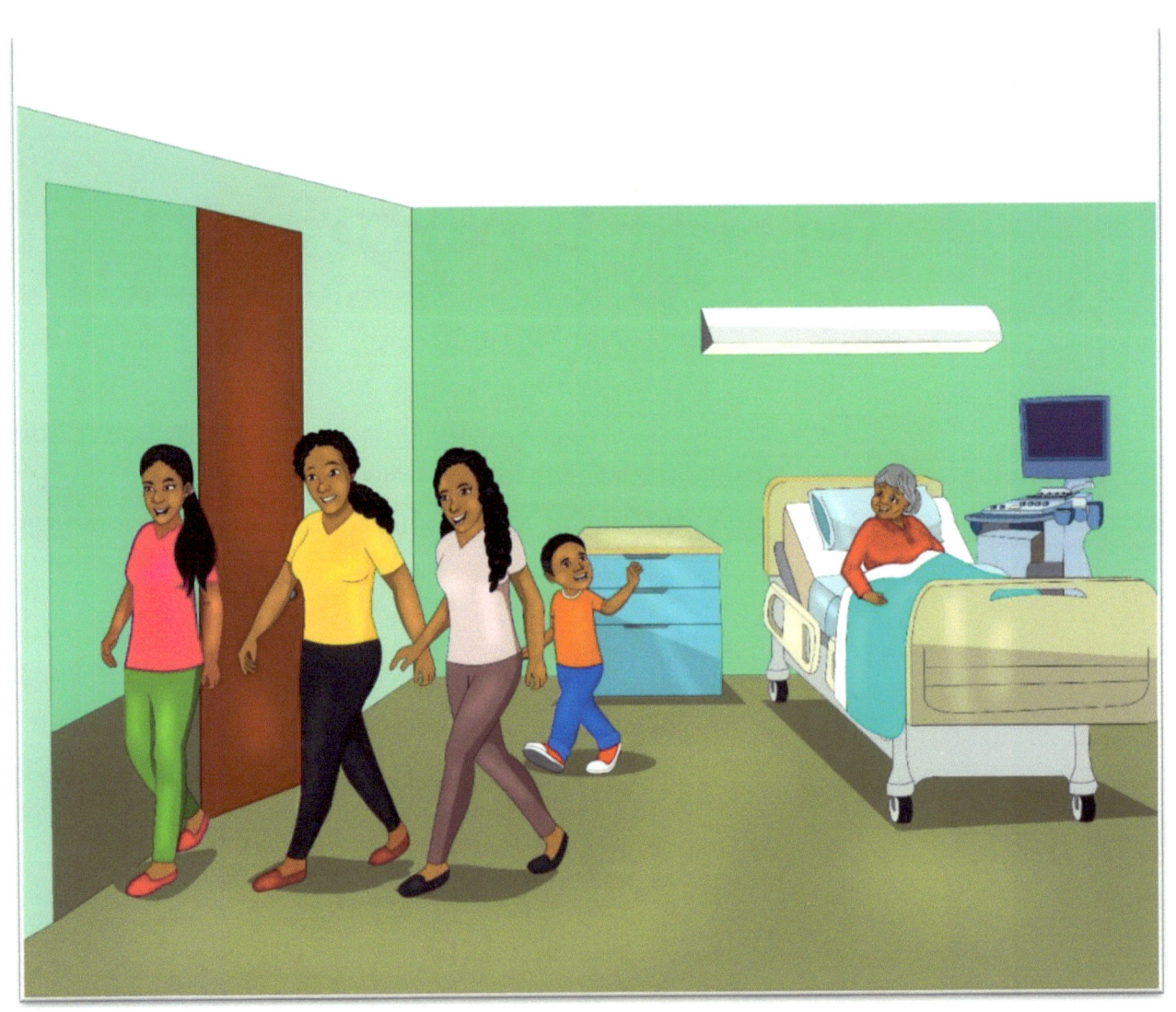

4

2. The Night I Met Jesus

Intercom comes on: Visiting hours are now over you may return tomorrow morning at 7 am.

Ok, grandmother I'll see you tomorrow!

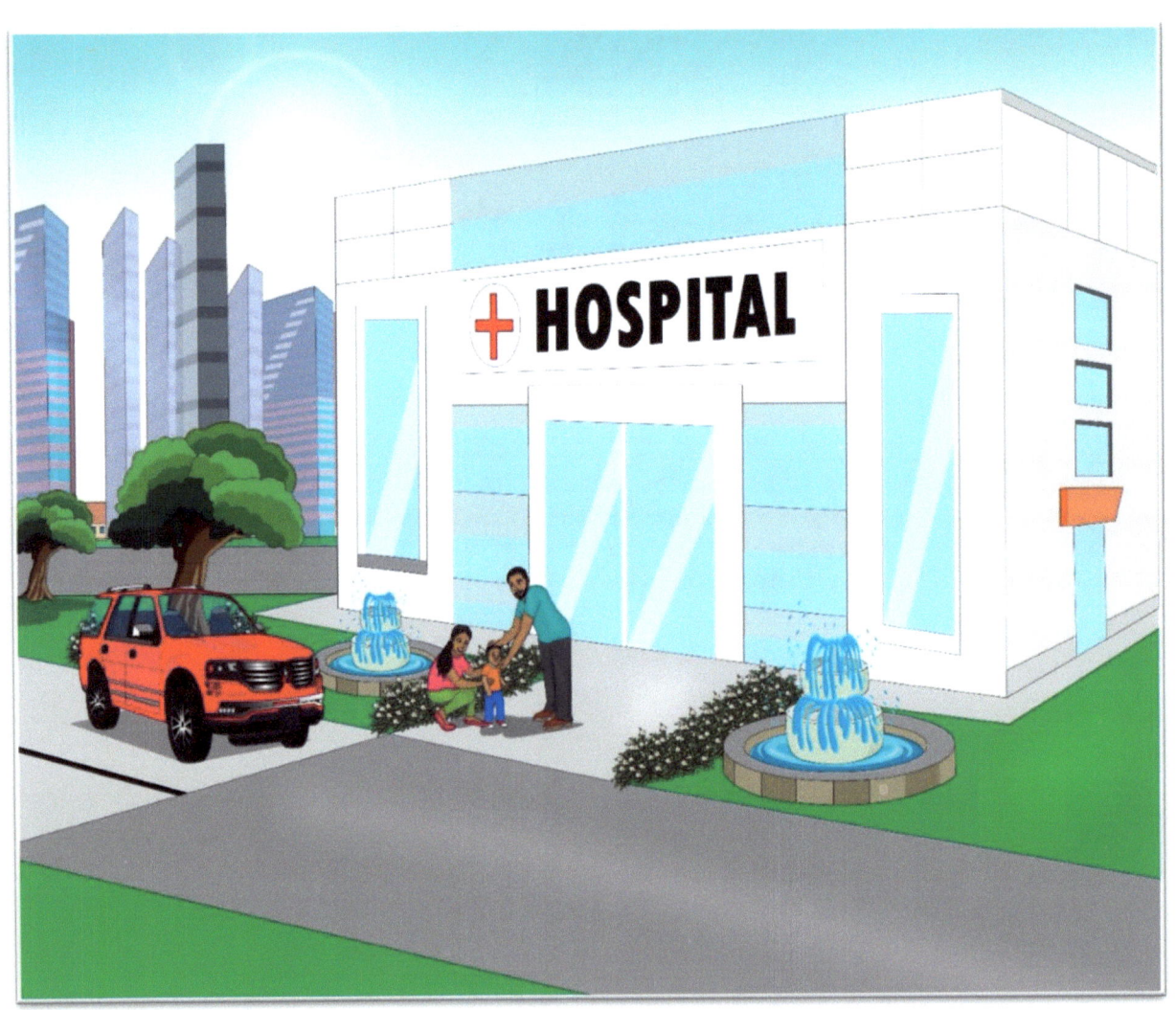

3. The Night I Met Jesus

As Sheldon walks away with his mother he starts to cry. Why are you crying Sheldon? his mother asked. I really want grandmother to come home! His mother quickly replied that she will come home, but she just needed to get better.

4. The Night I Met Jesus

Later that day, Sheldon's mom received a phone call. It was the hospital calling to inform the family that Sheldon's grandmother was not doing well, and they needed to get back to the hospital.

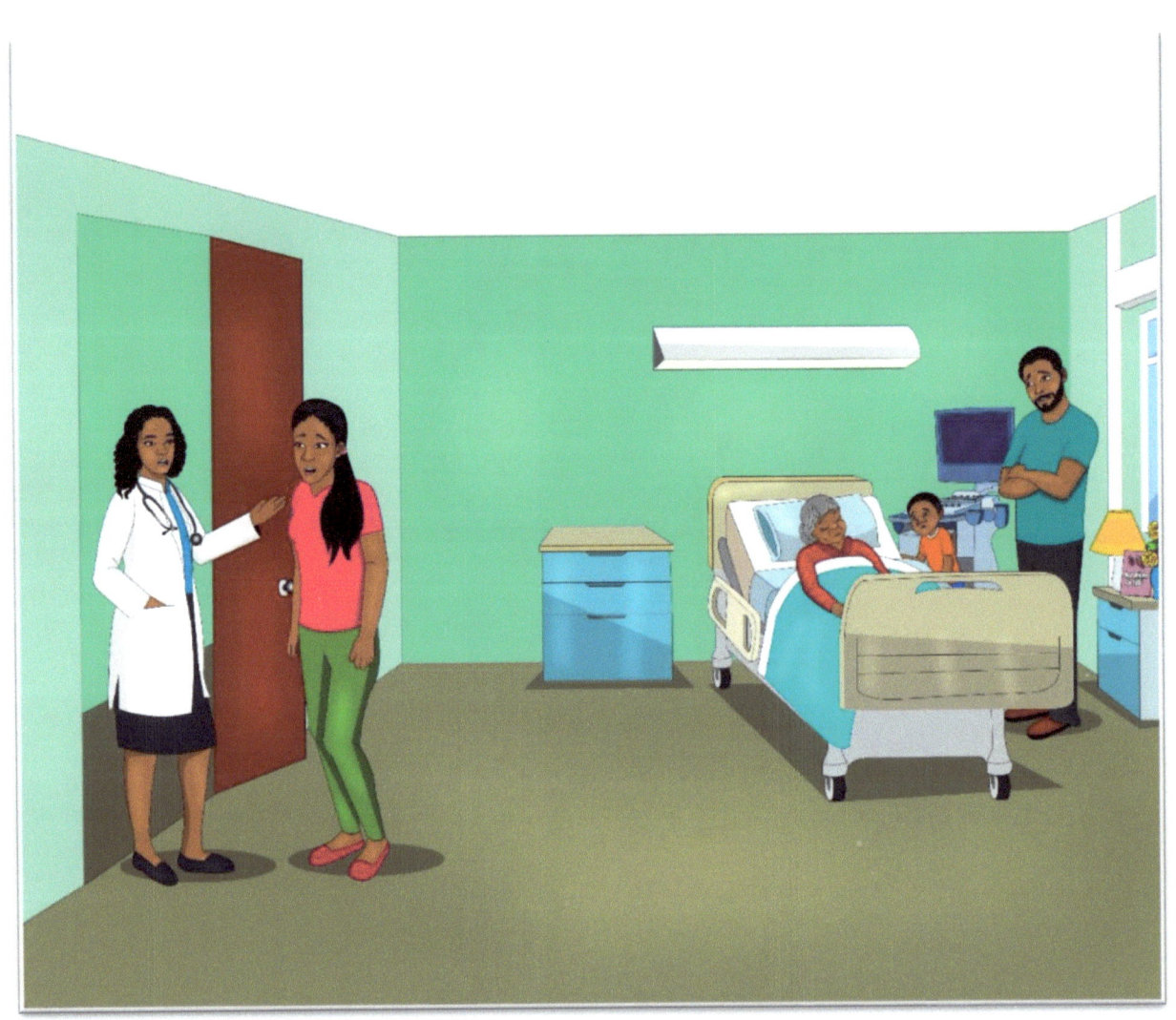

5. The Night I Met Jesus

When they arrived, his grandmother was not awake, her body was just lying there. Sheldon was very worried, and asked his mother what was wrong? His mother replied, "She fell into a light coma, which is a deep sleep and cannot wake up. "Oh, no"! Sheldon was very sad.

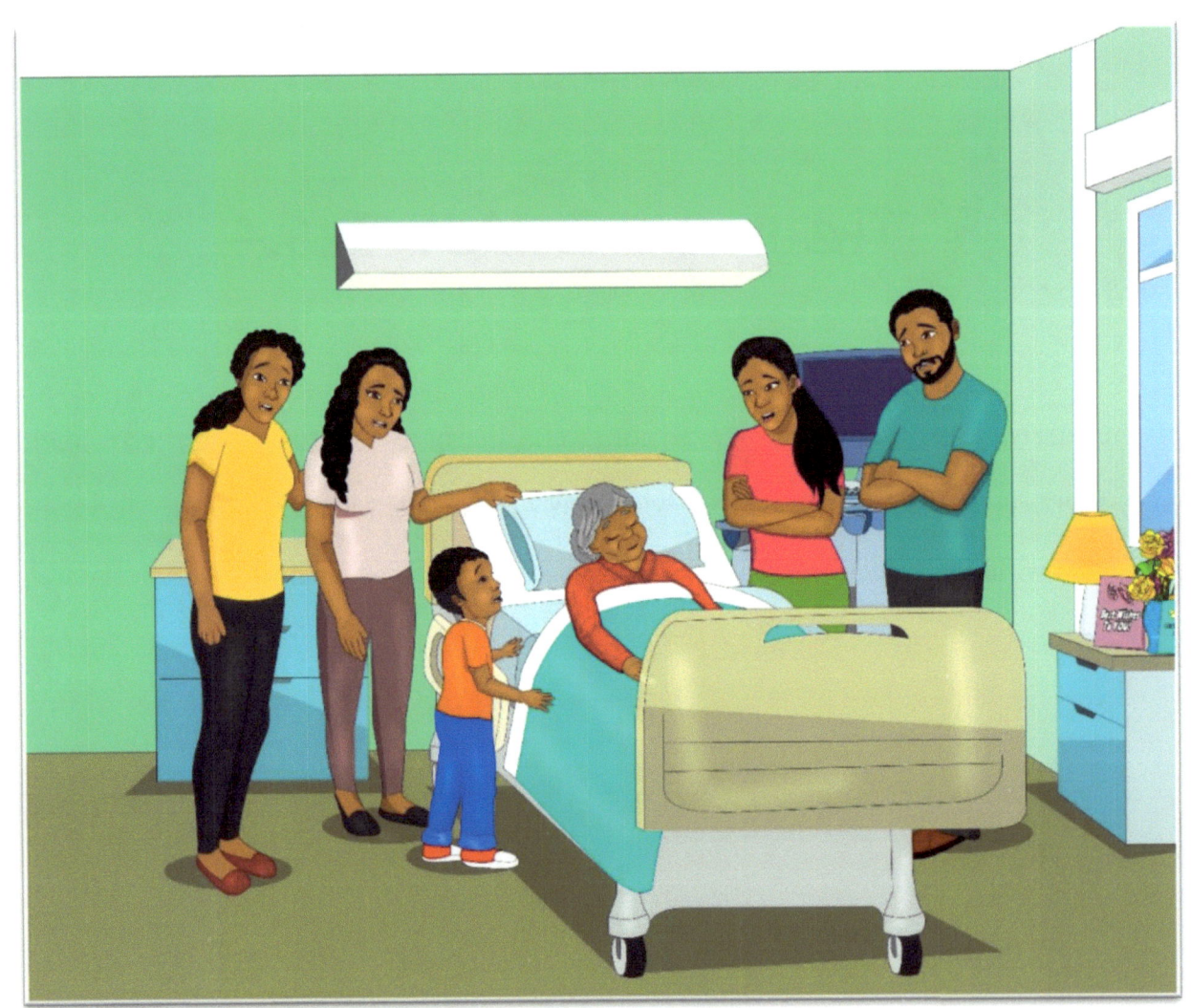

6. The Night I Met Jesus

As Aunt Tina and Aunt Stacy arrived at the hospital, Sheldon heard them say "Oh Jesus, please help our mother, oh merciful God!" Sheldon started wondering "Who is Jesus?"

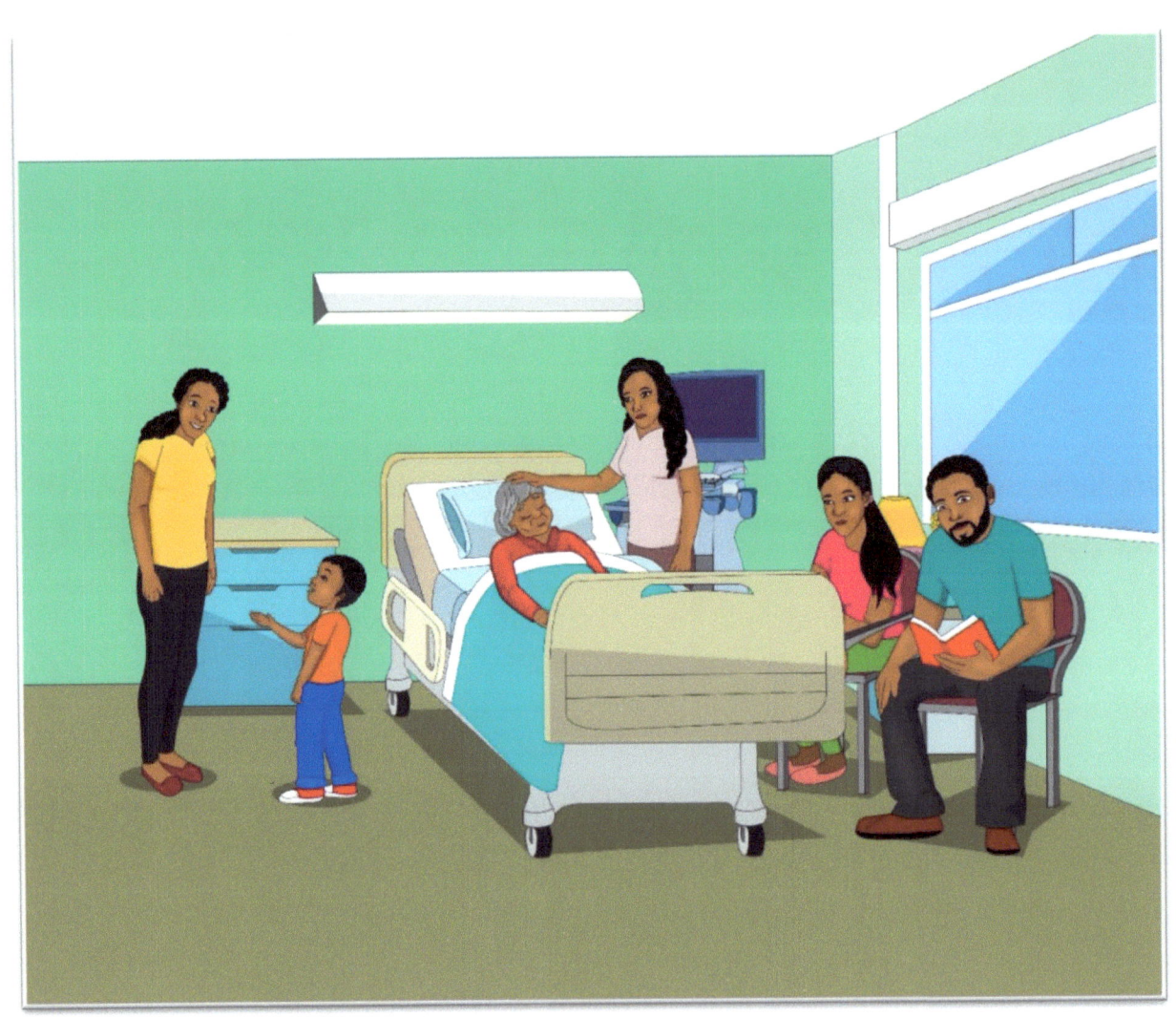

7. The Night I Met Jesus

Aunt Stacy who is this Jesus person she spoke about, and why mom didn't ask for him. Does she know this Jesus?

Aunt Stacy she smiled and replied, yes, your mother knows who He is, she just doesn't speak of Him anymore. You see, Sheldon, some years ago, before you were born, she prayed to Jesus to heal our dad, your grandfather, but he still passed away. She was very close to our dad, and ever since then she has developed a hardened heart for Jesus; that's why she does not speak of Him.

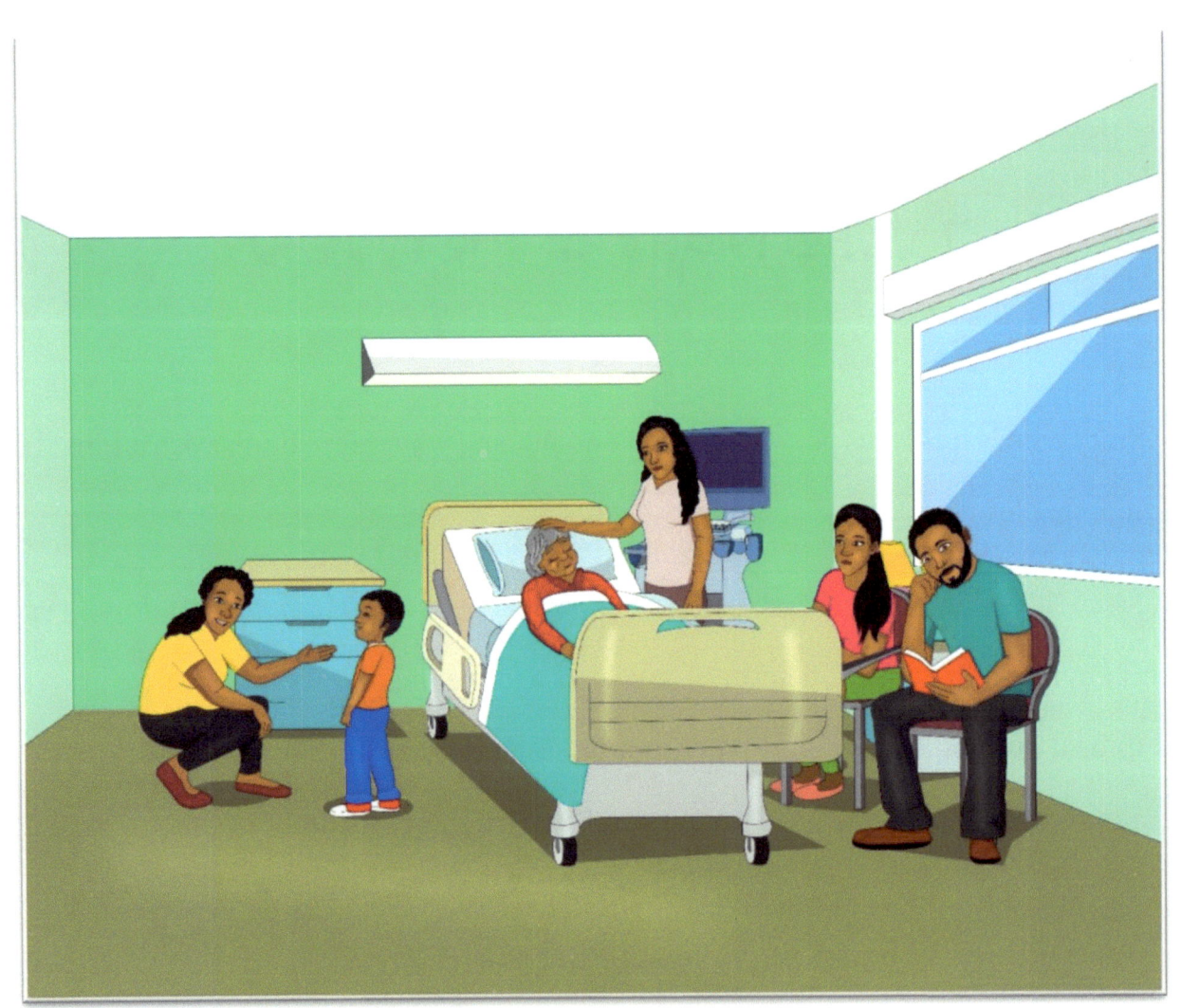

8. The Night I Met Jesus

So, is Jesus a doctor? Sheldon asked. Aunt Stacy was laughing and told him you can call Him that, and many other things, too. He is the Son of God, Jesus came to earth, and died for our sins and went back up to heaven, and if we believe in Him, we may have everlasting life

9. The Night I Met Jesus

If we are having any problems in life, we may go to Him because He is with us He will never leave nor forsake us, and if it's in His will all things shall come to pass.

"Sheldon wanted to know this Jesus, so His auntie explained that if you ask Him to come into your life, He will be there.

10. The Night I Met Jesus

Later that night, when Sheldon got home, he waited for the family to go to sleep. He began saying "I don't know you Jesus, but I would like to! I ask you to come into my life, and show me the way." As he finished his sentence, out of nowhere, a light appeared, and a voice said, "This is Jesus, I am here. I have always been with you'.

11. The Night I Met Jesus

As Sheldon smiled, there was this feeling of joy, happiness and comfort. Sheldon asked Jesus if he could heal his grandmother, because she had been very sick, and she wouldn't wake up.

"Hush, my child it has been done, "Jesus replied. He spent the rest of the night talking and laughing with Jesus, and they became good friends.

12. The Night I Met Jesus

The next morning, his mother was yelling "Wake up, wake up!" What's wrong, mom?" Sheldon asked My mother, your grandmother, is awake! She yelled with excitement. The family quickly got ready, and rushed to the hospital.

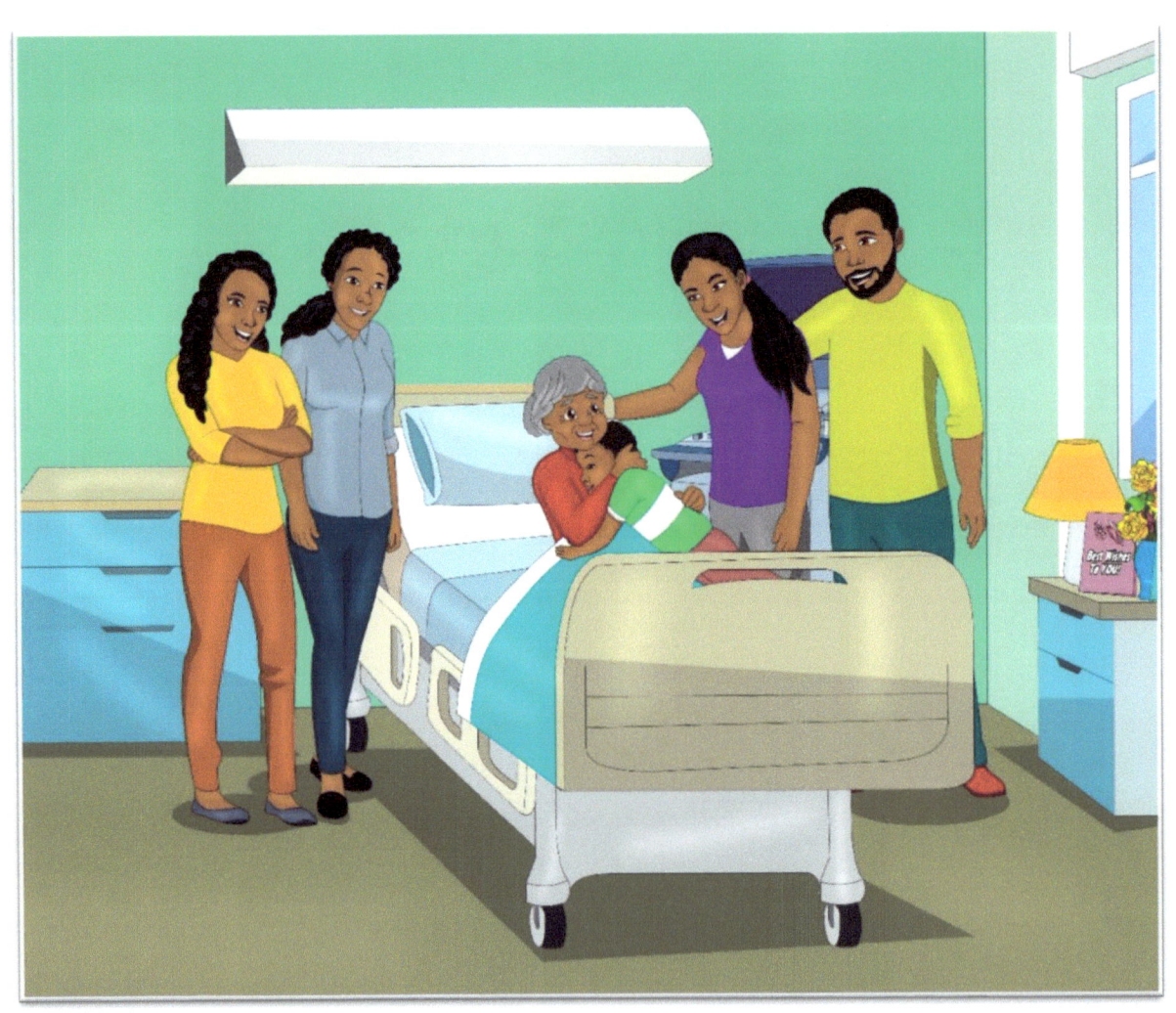

13. The Night I Met Jesus

As soon as they arrived, Sheldon saw she was awake, and ran over to give her a big hug. He could not wait to tell his grandmother, that he met Jesus the night before, and had asked Him to heal her.

14. The Night I Met Jesus

"Aunt Stacy, "I did exactly what you told me to do, and it worked! Aunt Stacy looking puzzled asked, "what are you talking about Sheldon?" "I'm talking about Jesus; Sheldon said" He was so happy and thankful. He said to her, "I went home last night, and asked Jesus to come into my life and He did!

15. The Night I Met Jesus

I also asked him to heal grandmother, and he did! We talked for a long time. Jesus told me, that I am very special to him, and that he loves me so much and that He would like to continue to be my friend.

16. The Night I Met Jesus

And mom, Jesus said, let not your heart be trouble for the night your father died! His will was done! He has never left you; He has always been with you! Sheldon's mom started to cry of happiness. She smiled with joy in her heart, and the room began to fill with joy, and everyone was giving praise to Jesus.

17. The Night I Met Jesus

Sheldon turned to his grandmother, and said, "I love you

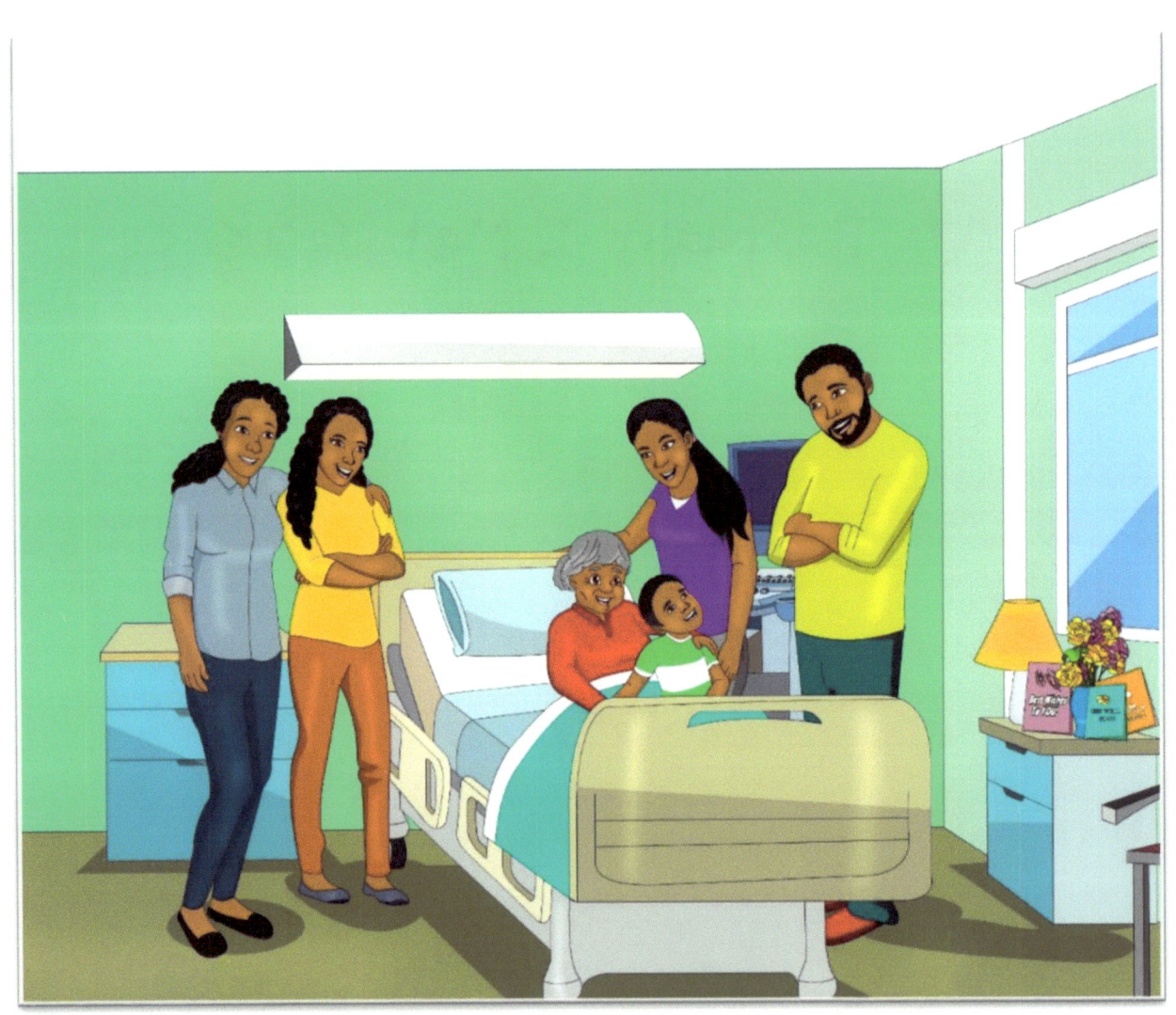

18. The Night I Met Jesus

And as he looked up to heaven he said, thank you Jesus…

THE END